A LITTLE LIGHT

POEMS

Coleman Glenn

Copyright © 2024 Coleman Glenn
All rights reserved.
ISBN: 979-8-218-51459-4

For Anne Grace. With all of my everything.

CONTENTS

Acknowledgements	xi
PART ONE: THE EVERYDAY	**1**
Syrup Season	3
Chicken Run	5
First Trimester	6
Diagnosis	7
For Deborah	8
A Triolet For Violet	9
For Beatrice	10
Precarious	11
Bears	12
Swing Kids	14
Sever's Disease	15
How To Ride the Waves	16
Antipodes	17
A Crowded House	18
Revision	19
Points Of Entry	20
Kitchen Signs	21
Decade: A Crown of Sonnets	22
Year One	22

Year Two	23
Year Three	24
Year Four	25
Year Five	26
Year Six	27
Year Seven	28
Year Eight	29
Year Nine	30
Year Ten	31

PART TWO: VERSE LIGHT AND DARK — 33

Fourth Trimester	35
The Fair Youth's Complaint	36
Stopping By Ikea on a Snowy Evening	37
The Shallows	38
Rubbernecking	39
State of the Union	40
Harmony of the Spheres	41
Coach Pitch	42
Subliminal Stimuli	43
Apocalypse	44
The Truth	45
Annoying People	46
Because What The World Needs Is Another Poem About Mowing	47
On the Third Anniversary of Obtaining a Trendy Kitchen Appliance	48
Marketing	49

When They Tell You to Get Your Act Together	50
Midlife Millenials	51
An Old Joke	52
Logic	53
I'll Be Back	54
(My Allergy's) Popular	55
The (Houston) Tiger	57
Definitely A Real Message from T-Mobile	58
The Fabric of Our Lives	59
Rondeau for the Southern Ocean	60
A Practical Solution	61
What Really Matters	62
PART THREE: DEVOTIONAL POEMS AND HYMNS	**63**
A Southern Christmas	65
A Cappella	66
How Long, O Lord	67
New Church Day	68
Hymn for a Baptism	69
Hymn for a Wedding	70
Labor of Love	71
How Just, How Learned, How Wise	72

Meditation on the Magnificat	75
Five Parables of Jesus	76
I. Parable of the Good Samaritan	76
II. Parable of the Sower	77
III. Parable of the Prodigal Son	78
IV. Parable of the Pharisee and the Publican	79
V. Parable of the Wheat and the Tares	80
Outer Darkness	81
Woe, Woe, Woe	82
Inheritance	83
Temptation	84
Palm Sunday	85
Ecce Homo	86
The Road to Emmaus	87
Vine and Branches	88
Starsong	89
The Least of These	90
Thanksgiving	91
About The Author	93

ACKNOWLEDGEMENTS

I am grateful to these publications for publishing the following poems, some of them in earlier versions:

Asses of Parnassus: "The Shallows"

Autumn Sky Poetry Daily: "Labor of Love," "Antipodes," "Rubbernecking," and "Syrup Season"

Blue Unicorn: "Points of Entry"

The Dirigible Balloon: "When They Tell You to Get Your Act Together…"

Grand Little Things: "Swing Kids" and "Precarious"

Light: "The Fair Youth's Complaint," "The (Houston) Tiger," "On the Third Anniversary of Obtaining a Trendy Kitchen Appliance," "Definitely a Real Message from T-Mobile," "The Fabric of Our Lives", "Rondeau for the Southern Ocean," and "What Really Matters."

New Church Life: "Palm Sunday," "Ecce Homo," and "The Road to Emmaus"

Theta Alpha Journal: "Temptation," "The Least of These," and "A Cappella"

THINK: "Diagnosis", "How to Ride the Waves", and "Bears"

Trinity House Review: "Chicken Run"

The Washington Post: "Marketing," "A Practical Solution," "Fourth Trimester", "I'll Be Back", and "Stopping by IKEA"

Poems from *The Washington Post* were published in the Style Invitational contest, now running simply as "The Invitational" in The Gene Pool newsletter on Substack.

Thanks to J-T Kelly for his helpful feedback on the manuscript.

PART ONE: THE EVERYDAY

SYRUP SEASON

Tromping through the sugar bush,
you reach the sugar shack,
where maple vapors, sugar-sweet,
seep out from every crack.

Within, your uncles, bleary-eyed,
are chatting man to man,
their fingers scorched from siphoning
hot sap from pan to pan.

On seeing you, they place a pail
and let the nectar flow
to fill the metal bucket
with an earthy amber glow.

A tea towel tops it to protect
the priceless stuff inside.
You've reached the age: you take the pail,
and try to almost glide

as carefully, so carefully
you tread the houseward way:
a muddy trail where last night's snow
melts into slush today.

400 meters, give or take.
It never felt so long.
Too slow, and it will get too cold;
too fast, with one foot wrong,

you'll spill a hundred dollars' worth
of syrup in the slurry
of almost-springtime forest muck.
So, gingerly you hurry,

and reach the door, then up the stairs,
to Nana in the kitchen
beside her boiling pots, who pours
your syrup, pure and rich, in.

The house is bright and rowdy, filled
with more than it can hold.
You'll let the syrup cool a bit,
then bottle liquid gold.

CHICKEN RUN

You saw them just before they crossed the road:
escapees in the yard, uncooped and gone
free-ranging — four hens foraging the lawn
for fallen berries buried in the mowed
mid-autumn grass. Love, you did not explode
or raise your voice or even touch upon
my failure to nail all the mesh back on.
Instead, you sent me for a bucketload
of chicken scratch, and with their favorite food
you slowly coaxed our ladies through the door.
Then, getting low and face-to-face you cooed
respectfully to them — just as before
you've often spoken to our other brood,
our flock about to grow from three to four.

FIRST TRIMESTER
For Anne Grace

You know that challenge on *Survivor* where
they step up to a floating platform's peak
and fight the waves to find their balance there?
By then, their brains and bodies are so weak
most drop. The holdouts struggle, breaker-tossed,
to keep their feet, stop swaying, just — hold still.
Imagine, now, if every time they lost
they could restart. A few might have the will
to persevere for — maybe half a day?
But somehow, you — as weeks and months expand
your seasick soul — ascend again and stay
unmoved until you cannot stand to stand.
The dull horizon where you fix your eyes
betrays no hint of any promised prize.

DIAGNOSIS

The good news is, no endometriosis.
I'd thought we'd find some, so I looked around
and your appendix — see, this picture here —
you see how white it is? It would have burst
in days. I called a colleague in; we cut
it out, along with this, a tiny growth
I noticed on your lower pelvic wall.
Pathology results came yesterday.
There were two tumors: one that filled the whole
of your appendix, one metastasis.
They're known as "carcinoid." It's very rare.
Forgive me, I've been reading up all night.
It is malignant. Cancer, yes. I'm sorry.
It moves more slowly than most cancers do,
but still... I wish I could say more but this
is not my field; I have no way to tell

that in a month you'll leave this continent;
that two months after that a surgery
will leave you bleeding out and clutching death —
that you will watch as others watch your kids
while your recovery drags on for months
and years, until you reach a slowly rising
stasis where your days are filled again
with small annoyances and snorted laughs
and arguments and reconciliations,
and then a baby girl, her birth at home
a miracle of muscle and God's grace,
the outpour of a body that will work,
whatever demons lurk within its walls.

So send back word, please, when five years from now
you labor yet again, and let me know
how life is going on as life goes on.

FOR DEBORAH

Deb·o·rah, noun: a female given name: from the Hebrew "D'vorah," meaning "bee"

Dear one, a week before you came
Each blossom on the cherry tree
Began to hum your hidden name
Out loud in honeyed harmony.

Recalling this I listen now
And revel in your newborn song:
Huge sighs as tiny lungs allow,
Grunts, cries, and milk-calls sweet and strong.

As all your snuffled sounds subside,
Eliding into easy breath,
Long shadows fill the lawn outside,
Grown green and wild past winter's death.

Lie still, my daughter, on my chest;
Embrace this slumber peacefully.
New dreams are stirring while you rest,
New tiny wings of what might be.

A TRIOLET FOR VIOLET

With dewy drops on velvet skin
this springlike February day,
your life in sunlight will begin
with dewy drops on velvet skin.
Your perfect eyelids, petal-thin,
dip down and lift like flowers at play
with dewy drops on velvet skin
this springlike February day.

FOR BEATRICE

"Come, oh Sleep; come, oh Sleep; come to where my child is, Sleep." — from Sumerian cradlesong Šulgi N, on tablet UM 29-16-85 in the Penn Museum

Beside the Penn Museum's brown brick walls
Extend the hospitals. Here you are held
Above smooth streets where city traffic crawls.

Today, since being born, you've been propelled
Repeatedly to planes of higher light
In which what's in and out no longer meld —

Caught in our hands at home in waning night,
Emerging into early morning air,
Then whisked to here, where everything seems bright.

Give in, blessed child, to Mama's calming care.
Let sleep come close and shut your widened eye.
Embrace her chest; hear heartbeat music there.

Next door a mother's words in clay long dry
Now sing a still and silent lullaby.

PRECARIOUS

She's at the age of scrapes and bruises;
edges seem to find her face.
The floor beneath her feet refuses
not to wobble out of place.

She's at the age of tears to laughter,
chortling through blood and drool,
careening onward moments after
diving off a three-foot stool.

She's at the age of near disaster,
toddling the precipice.
The tragedies keep whizzing faster
past. They graze her as they miss.

BEARS

My daughter says she's scared of bears.
I hesitate, then hew
to reassuring partial truths
("They're more afraid of you…").

My mind is in Alberta, though;
I knew a farmer there
who told me after church one Sunday
how he'd met a bear.

That Thursday he'd been walking up
a fairly narrow gap
between two fenced-in bison fields—
effectively a trap

when stoppered by a bear ahead.
It charged him without warning.
The farmer didn't always bring
his shotgun, but this morning,

he had it. Hoisting it, he fired —
misfired, only a click.
He pumped and fired again — a bang.
The second shot was quick,

but had he missed? The bear kept coming.
Just ten feet away,
it dropped. The man, at last, exhaled.
That Sunday, he would say

it took some time to realize
how close he'd come to death:
a trigger's width between his and
the black bear's final breath.

His father and his uncles who
had cleared the land he farmed
would not go near a bear by choice,
not even fully armed.

They never hid their healthy dread,
despite their winking stories.
I hear them when my daughter shares
her bear-related worries

and I, a grown suburbanite,
dismiss her primal fears
behind a blindness not afforded
kids or pioneers.

SWING KIDS

Just a couple of boys on the swings
talking seven-year-old things:
favorite Pokémon,
what part of Zelda they're on,
stuff they both like to do outside,
good places to hide,
what schools they were at
when the virus arrived. Things like that,
like this chat
doesn't come as the first of its kind in a year,
like parents' fear
can be shed like an oversized coat —
like if launched from the swings, they'd float.

SEVER'S DISEASE

Sever's disease (also known as calcaneal apophysitis) is one of the most common causes of heel pain in growing children. (American Academy of Orthopaedic Surgeons).

For Eleanor

It's often found in kids who grow
by leaps above their closest peers,
whose bones pretend that months are years
but fail to let the tendons know.

You juggle three bowls and a plate
while chasing both the little ones.
Like you, your childhood skips and runs.
You'll soar – but you're allowed to wait.

HOW TO RIDE THE WAVES

For Samuel

I over-coached you, saying way too much
about exactly where your hands should go
and how far up the board to scooch, with such
precision you'd already have to know
the feeling to begin to practice it.
You caught a broken breaker anyway
and rode it all the way to land, face lit
with revelation as you split the spray.

"I did it!" you called out as you splashed back
to me. "I love it! It's like — at the start
I got the tingles, just like when I whack
my funny bone, without the hurting part.
It felt so good!" All afternoon you caught
the waves, thrown off by some, sticking enough
to carry you to evening, when we brought
our things back up before it got too rough.

All that was yesterday; today you test
the surf, waiting with me until you spy
a good one coming close about to crest
and fling yourself aboard, balancing high
atop its sliding cliff before you tip
over the edge and cruise across the clear
saltwater glass in front of it. You slip
to shore, and there you are, and I'm out here.

ANTIPODES

Thick snow fell the November he was born,
before we moved a hemisphere away
and she arrived one January morning,
crying to ignite the summer day.

He's seven now, and this month she's still five —
an artificial gap for kids so near
in size, in schemes, in love for things alive;
who hear, "Are you two twins?" more every year.

But she — she sings her world into existence,
narrating every heartbreak, every high;
elaborating epics with insistence
that this is real, that fairies are nearby.

He, too, dreams deep, builds Lego worlds, pretends;
he shouts his news to strangers when he's proud.
But precious things he shelters and defends;
he often prays but seldom prays aloud.

And yet, the pair are partners in one story,
twined threads within a tapestry unfurled
by what they say or hide of grief and glory;
two sides of the same half-illumined world.

A CROWDED HOUSE

It's four a.m. Our seven-year-old son
just heaved up bile into the plastic bin
I grabbed out of his sisters' room at one.
(The barely-better two-year-old gave in
to sleep again a little after three.)
This bug already wracked the rest of us:
the six-year-old last week; my wife and me,
my live-in in-laws, all in synchronous
attacks two days ago. Our strength still drained,
our joints and muscles aching, we are past
fatigue. Too soon, we'll wake up foggy-brained
to tend this boy whose fitful sleep won't last.
Time melts as I sink back. No one can measure
how far the fullness here surpasses pleasure.

REVISION

Their clumsiness annoys me. No,
their carelessness. Their choice
to rush. I yelled. But really though,
I barely raised my voice.

POINTS OF ENTRY

I want to know which kid forgot to close
the chickens' nesting boxes yesterday,
exposing all the birds for helpless prey
to any predator with half a nose.
I want to know what time somebody chose
to let them out into the yard to play
then didn't think to put them back away
and latch the door against their frequent foes.

I want to know which route the fox took in
to start his early morning savagery —
not that it matters; either way'd have been
cut off last night if I'd gone out to see.
I want to know when error turned to sin;
I want to know this isn't all on me.

KITCHEN SIGNS

An unembodied oven mitt
that grips an iron handle;
up on the stool, triumphantly,
a long-lost purple sandal;
a pile of pants and dirty rags
beside the basement door —
a language born of accidents
to mend what's come before.

DECADE: A CROWN OF SONNETS

Year One

Like endless vines that spring from simple seeds,
eternal things begin in finite time.
A moment ruptures; from its heart proceeds
a living shoot, enduring and sublime.
And so it was, ten years ago today,
when from our parted lips emerged, "I will,"
that fragile walls between us fell away
and our two separate souls began to spill
into a vessel surer than its parts,
a union that would not be put asunder,
a wreathing of our bodies, minds, and hearts
which, in a burst of ordinary wonder,
would rise from roots sunk deep into the earth
to reach another soul's embodied birth.

Year Two

To reach *another* soul's embodied birth
we semi-circumnavigate the globe,
arriving in the manse at 30 Perth,
your belly growing round beneath your robe.
A world away from continents we've known,
we've moved from moose to monkeys on the lawn
(minuter creatures, notably more prone
to grabbing fruit from counters when we're gone).
We make the typical mistakes: drive on the right,
assume a hadeda's a screaming child,
trip motion sensors in the lounge at night,
prepare for Christmas weather to be mild.
But strangers turn to friends; in half a year,
although we've left a home, home finds us here.

Year Three

Although we've left a home, home finds us here
attempting to construct a four-square frame
of everyday routine, to engineer
a habitat the four of us can claim.
We dig a fresh foundation in the clay
of New Church Westville's dense community,
stack bricks of chaplain's work and Godly Play,
put up a roof of steady constancy.
It isn't perfect – often there's a mess,
and frequently we have to make repairs,
remodeling our hours to handle stress;
but we're content with how our household fares.
We don't detect the fault about to bring
the earthquake that will topple everything.

Year Four

The earthquake that will topple everything
begins with warning tremors in your health:
decreasing weight, sharp pains, a steady string
of dizzy spells whose source persists in stealth.
Exploratory surgery ("routine")
explodes with vivid images of truth:
tumors, whose size and scope can only mean
they've infiltrated since your early youth.
Flung back across the world, you undergo
another knife, an almost-death, a loss
of blood and bowel and everything you know
of what's to come. But carrying this cross,
you're carried when the canyons gape too broad:
on darkest nights, you glimpse the light of God.

Year Five

On darkest nights, you glimpse the light of God;
in dismal afternoons, our eyes are dimmer,
as missteps show how thoroughly we're flawed
and make it hard to catch the former glimmer.
Still, motes of sunshine filter through the cloud:
a Broadway show that spotlights friendly souls;
a move assisted by a cheerful crowd;
a meeting where you sense potential roles.
These don't eliminate the thick malaise
and sullen silence threatening to smother
our flame that falls when by our thoughtless ways
and careless words we sometimes wound each other.
But they're sufficient in the slowest slog
to help us find a pathway through the fog.

Year Six

To help us find a pathway through the fog
that cloaks each symptom and its origin,
you let physicians poke and scan and log
where tumors end and drug effects begin.
They don't find much, and when they do, they waffle:
you bleed because your blood is slow to clot,
which tells us why your surgeries were awful
— except for once or twice when they were not.
So many of the tests are borderline —
for SVT, for platelets, for arthritis,
for tumors and stenosis in your spine.
How beautifully clear the test that night is
when, crying out and laughing, halfway wild
you tell me we've conceived another child.

Year Seven

You tell me we've conceived another child;
we hope, this time, to welcome her at home,
but midwives balk at paperwork we've filed.
With one trimester left, we quickly comb
our mental list of birth-adjacent friends,
gathering threads of knowledge and assistance
we'll need before week thirty-seven ends —
in part for you, but more for my resistance
as, overwhelmed, I try to piece together
a patchwork understanding that will hold
through what emergencies we'll have to weather
if any of my pent-up fears unfold.
But, smoothing out my ruffled mind, you bear
with peace you have received and freely share.

Year Eight

With peace you have received and freely share
we prep for a pandemic, mostly calm,
although our global ties make us aware
how little time is left before the bomb.
No strangers to a catastrophic shock,
we huddle in our bunker when it hits
and check in on the wider family flock
remotely, staying put till risk permits.
With everybody else, we read the news
of illnesses and death; with them, we weep.
This isolation isn't what we'd choose,
but we are spared a penalty more steep.
The onslaught ebbs and flows; beyond each surge
we savor freedom more when we emerge.

Year Nine

We savor freedom more when we emerge
from claustrophobic winter into spring
and finally can satisfy the urge
to chat with neighbors while our children swing.
The virus isn't gone, but we have learned
to move around it, finding open air.
Community in person has returned
with caution and considerable care.
The springtime brings, as well, a brighter blessing:
an April baby, lively as a bee,
her giggles and her cries alike expressing
the openness and trust of infancy.
And even when the newness starts to wane
we catch the scent of sweet and cleansing rain.

Year Ten

We catch the scent of sweet and cleansing rain;
late summer haziness begins to turn
to autumn's sharper air. The woods remain
a haven where our children roam and learn.
It's probable we've taken on too much:
expectant, teaching lessons (you outdoors),
plus parenting. We still find ways to touch.
A big kid helps a little one with chores.
A sister greets her brother with a hug.
We walk with friends; we give their kids a ride;
they do the same. Our family's safe and snug.
Each morning I wake up beside my bride.
The small things grow to answer all our needs
like endless vines that spring from simple seeds.

PART TWO: VERSE LIGHT AND DARK

FOURTH TRIMESTER

"Fourth trimester, n.: the three month period immediately following giving birth in which the mother typically recovers from childbirth and adjusts to caring for her infant" (Merriam-Webster)

We cuddled you close for the whole fourth trimester —
we cherished that bond, and the closeness was heaven.
And dear, we still love you; we don't mean to pester —
but . . . leave. It's trimester one hundred and seven.

THE FAIR YOUTH'S COMPLAINT
An Imagined Reply to Shakespeare's "Procreation Sonnets"

Well, Bill, your sonnets finally got to me,
With all their pressures to impress my seal
On waxen fruits that fruit eternally,
Et cetera, so forth, you know the spiel.
Enticed by your advice I grabbed a wife
With features fairly fine but not so strong
That they might mask my own engrafted life,
So sweetly celebrated in your song.
She birthed a boy. I staked and pruned him well;
I snipped and shaped his soul to match my own.
He blossomed, and I watched my own pride swell
Within a youth in whom my luster shone.
But oh, he burst, and spattered *me* with scorn!
Such bitter fruit were better left unborn.

STOPPING BY IKEA ON A SNOWY EVENING

"In northern Denmark, an IKEA showroom turned into a vast bedroom. Six customers and about two dozen employees were stranded by a snowstorm and spent the night in the store, sleeping in the beds that are usually on show."
—Associated Press

(with apologies to Robert Frost)

Whose store this is we surely know;
Head office is in Stockholm, though.
They will not mind us staying here
As all the roads fill up with snow.

With suppertime now drawing near
We have provisions for good cheer,
E.g., a lingonberry shake
With Swedish meatballs and a beer.

Then after dinner we can take
A showroom bed—no need to make
This furniture, no need to keep
That tool to fix some dumb mistake.

The beds, it's true, are kind of cheap;
But dreams of doing this run deep,
And where else would we rather sleep?
There's nowhere else we'd rather sleep.

THE SHALLOWS

His smile is like a lighthouse in the dark
that flashes *here find shipwreck and the shark.*

RUBBERNECKING

Beyond the median, a crumpled frame,
police lights, acrid smoke. So now it's clear
why two miles back the interstate became
a shuffling carpet queued for a premiere.
I try to keep my gaze ahead; with luck,
delays like this will soon be obsolete,
when cruise control puts every car and truck
on track in steady progress down the street,
immune to horror's all-too-human hold
on those who cannot help but slow and see;
creating distance, comforting and cold,
from the appalling possibility
that vehicles on both sides of the line
contain, in fragile flesh, lives just like mine.

STATE OF THE UNION

Our revolution wasn't one
whose ends required a guillotine.
Our civil war was waged between
states set before the war was done.
Our breaks and sutures have been clean,
at least as imaged on a chart;
there may be something in the heart
whose tendency remains unseen.

HARMONY OF THE SPHERES

For MBS

The sense that comes from looking up at night
of being less than infinitesimal
comes over me in daylight hours as well
when, listening for something out of sight,

I lean into the points of background noise
that I can't simultaneously hold:
out on the driveway, gravel being rolled
inside the wheels of plastic riding toys;

close by, the fridge's hum, its mid-range voice
one strand in a discordant throbbing choir
of lawnmower and jet and fan and dryer.
The white noise pixelates with every choice.

I'm drawn in to this kind of listening
by catching on a sound I've missed before
that's surely common: footfalls on the floor
above an empty duct re-echoing;

a keening that must be the baby's cry
resolved once I am halfway down the hall
into a pop song muffled by a wall;
a rumbling, tiny diesel driving by;

a subtle oddness of pronunciation
that turns the words which follow into blabber;
a startled squirrel's chirping jibber jabber.
I half-hear hints of some vast revelation.

COACH PITCH

The pitcher/coach repeats the common lie:
"Just one more swing. OK, *one* more, last one."
It's only fair — these girls should get to try
until they've hit; they're out here to have fun.
Besides, "one more" means one unerring pitch,
one ball precisely placed to catch a bat,
one toss with aim and timing to bewitch
a no-look swing to drive a softball flat.

Above his own refrain, above the cries
of players spelling out a practiced cheer,
above his on-deck daughter's drawn-out sighs,
the coach, persistent, also seems to hear
a whispering from bleachers out of view:
If this kid whiffs, her heartache is on you.

SUBLIMINAL STIMULI

Blips too abrupt to capture consciously
Enchant you, planting seeds of new desire —
So goes the story. In reality,
These cues nudge latent wants a smidgen higher,

Supporting choices you've already made.
Or, oftener, they don't do much at all.
No adman pushing nuts and lemonade,
No brainwasher who plots a country's fall,
Exerts control through millisecond flashes.
The myth persists; it whispers you might find

Excusing factors when commitment crashes,
Veiled saboteurs who've undermined your mind.
Evading notice in plain sight, meanwhile,
Real motives amble, dressed in bare denial.

APOCALYPSE

If sunshine filters through the solid gray
to warm the muggy earthbound air today,
that air, on sensing that it's been set free,
will rouse itself and rise up suddenly
past stratus clouds that hang in disarray

to heights where, in an aerial ballet
of atmospheric clash and interplay,
the sky will roil to black opacity —
if sunshine filters through.

Then limbs will snap and burly oaks will sway;
then lightning bolts will crack the dark of day
and thunder crush the silence, while a sea,
born instantly of instability,
crashes to earth. The stillness will not stay
if sunshine filters through.

THE TRUTH

Most things most people think are true
are true. Most grass is mostly green;
the sky, when clear, is mostly blue.
Most things most people think are true?
Not quite — thought burns for something new
outshining truth's unburnished sheen.
Most things most people think are true
are true. Most grass is mostly green.

ANNOYING PEOPLE

The roommate who cuts onions
on the common cutting board;
the snoozer who refuses
to believe that she just snored;
the colleague on the conference call
who never mutes his mic;
the outdoors type who won't shut up
about his latest hike;
the blabbermouth who keeps on talking
after saying "bye";
the snoop who always speculates
when someone meets a guy.
All bad, these bothers, but the worst
is not the folks who gab; it's
the ones who criticize me for
my harmless little habits.

BECAUSE WHAT THE WORLD NEEDS IS ANOTHER POEM ABOUT MOWING

Whoever mowed left tufts of grass
around odd objects on each pass,
endowing with a verdant halo
a baseball glove, a doll that lay low,
a rock, a stick, a crumpled dress.
Whoever mowed here must possess
a poet's soul and eye, to see
such glory in mundanity.
("Or he's just lazy"? Don't I know it —
perhaps you've never met a poet.)

ON THE THIRD ANNIVERSARY OF OBTAINING A TRENDY KITCHEN APPLIANCE

The instant that my Instant Pot
cast off its cardboard cradle,
once I'd removed the plastic junk
(a paddle and a ladle),

I made myself a solemn vow:
"This countertop behemoth
shall ever cook two meals a week
and gleam as now it gleameth."

I know: you think that in a month
my best-laid plans had busted,
that in a year the gadget sat
neglected and bedusted.

You're right. But I have won the war
despite that losing battle:
still almost every day I use
that ladle or that paddle.

MARKETING

An "air fryer's" really an oven — it
will not fry a thing that you shove in it.
I have tried the same lie —
"This spud tastes like a fry!"—
but I can't trick my kids into lovin' it.

WHEN THEY TELL YOU TO GET YOUR ACT TOGETHER

Get your act together:
congregate your clowns;
summon your assistants —
give them gaudy gowns.

Fetch your feathered flippers,
mount your mottled cow —
cry to all your critics,
"My act's together now!"

MIDLIFE MILLENIALS

I'm middle-aged, but crisis? Nah –
I feel no need to broadcast
my wealth or popularity.
Oh – do check out my podcast!

AN OLD JOKE

A rabbit, a priest, and a monk from back east
sauntered into a dingy saloon
where in no time at all they were caught in a brawl
over who played Will Kane in *High Noon*.
When the gun smoke had cleared the poor rabbit appeared
to have taken a shot in the knee.
Someone shouted, "Transfusion!", but in the confusion
Doc brought only types A and B.
When the rabbit was told, he complained, "I grow cold,
and as much as I'd rather not gripe, oh,
it's curtains, my friends; this is how it all ends;
I am just an unfortunate type O."

LOGIC

I guess leopards aren't too careful —
based on shepherds and their sheep,
a leopard, one assumes, must always
look after its leap.

I'LL BE BACK
(To the tune of "You'll Be Back" from Hamilton*)*

You say
I shouldn't have made any sequels beyond "Judgment Day."
You sigh,
As I trot out another one, "Why won't this cyborg just die?"
If they're bad,
Still the bling that they bring tends to jingle in quite a nice way.
It's the best role I've had:
Mechanical acting's a plus for the part that I play,
So…
I'll be back, like before
For some cockamamie future war.
I'll be back; terminate
Any hope there won't be seven or eight.
Profits rise, profits fall;
I get paid regardless through it all,
So despite all the flak,
Though they claim they've killed the series, don't be shocked if I come back.

Da da da dat da, dat da da da da ya da
Da da dat dat da ya da!
Da da da dat da, dat da da da da ya da
Da da dat dat da.

(MY ALLERGY'S) POPULAR
(*To the tune of "Popular" from* Wicked)

Whenever I'd eat somewhere
Less circumspect than I
(And let's face it — who wasn't
Less circumspect than I?)
I'd truly strain
To explain my need.
And if someone offered casserole
Or kindly tried to pass a roll
I'd groan to know how hard I was to feed.
And even if the place
Had heard of other cases with my case
They'd never have a clue how to proceed.
But fashions breed
At lightning speed
And. Now. It's

Popular!
My allergy's popular!
Now every celebrity
Wants to be like me
And eschew the foods I shun;
Now suddenly grocery aisles
Are well-stocked for miles —
Options throng where there were none

'Cause it's popular.
It's nice that it's popular.
Regardless, I have to wince
When a waiter hints
He abstains but tends to cheat;
What's that mean
For all of this stuff I'm about to eat?

I once experienced uncomprehending looks;
Now it seems like all I face is condescending looks:
To claim aversions that are lately trending looks
A little phony,

Smells like haute baloney.
So, even though it's popular,
I'm not feeling popular.
You've gotta take good with bad
When your fear's a fad;
When you feed me, I aver
That if I try to stop you,
It ain't because it's popular.

La la la la
My allergy is
Pop-u-lar.

When I get a bit less cautious
Oftentimes I end up nauseous;
Even if they've left the culprit out
There's still the
Chance for cross-contamination;
Hyper-thorough sanitation
Is not a thing most people
Care much about —

It's not popular.
Imagine how popular
To frequently second-guess
Your host's carefulness;
Try it, folks, and you can be
Very very popular
Like me.

And though, sick all night,
I could bring to light
Just what it does to me,
My friends say not to share it
Despite its popularity.

La la la la
It's so popular —
Just not quite as popular
With me.

THE (HOUSTON) TIGER

"Houston investigators said exotic animal traffickers are likely moving a suddenly famous tiger around from person to person to conceal its exact location."
—*Newsweek*

(with apologies to William Blake)

Tiger, tiger, lately loosed on
Lawns and alleyways of Houston;
What base thug's menagerie
Now holds thee in captivity?

In what villain's pen or shed
Dost thou lay thy fearful head?
Who so foolish as to cage
Thy crouching form of righteous rage?

What the prison, what the chain
Might this criminal restrain?
Is he soon to pace a cell
As cold as where thou now dost dwell?

Or – will he attempt to flee?
Will he, while on the lam, face thee?
Will he find a soft, warm place
From whence his smile grows on thy face?

Tiger, tiger, lately loosed on
Lawns and alleyways of Houston;
What base thug's menagerie
Dare hold thee in captivity?

DEFINITELY A REAL MESSAGE FROM T-MOBILE

"Scammers are targeting T-Mobile customers through a new ... text message [that] says that you may have been affected by a T-Mobile service outage and that the company wants to compensate you for the inconvenience." —BestLife

We much regret, dear customer,
the outage (which did not occur).
Moreover, we apologize
for slanders, insults, jabs, and lies
that you've endured throughout your life—
we now confess: we caused that strife.
In fact, the least thing that's gone wrong
for you was our fault all along.
To make it right, we're offering
a gift card. It's a little thing,
but please accept it as a token
of penance for the trust we've broken.
We know you're smart. You sniff scams out.
But there's no need for probing doubt
in this case. Let us overload you
with righteous lust for what is owed you.

THE FABRIC OF OUR LIVES

"'There's a trend in New York right now where people are wearing merch: carrying totes from local delis, hardware stores or their favorite steakhouse...' It turns out the wholehearted embrace of cotton totes may actually have created a new problem. An organic cotton tote needs to be used 20,000 times to offset its overall impact of production."
—*The New York Times*

In Brooklyn Heights the height of *haute*
couture includes a cotton tote
with logos from a local shop—
but soon, some say, this fad must stop.
The carbon costs of growing cotton
offset what gains the world has gotten
from cutting back on cheapo plastic.
Today the true iconoclastic
shopper won't use bags at all
but arms alone—although, recall
those local shops whose names adorned
the bags. Must these boutiques be scorned?
No! They'll be thrilled to offer you
a free, on-brand, bespoke tattoo.

RONDEAU FOR THE SOUTHERN OCEAN

"For the first time in the more than 100 years that the National Geographic Society has mapped the world's oceans, it will recognize five of them. The organization announced this week that it will recognize the Southern Ocean, a body of water that encircles Antarctica, as the world's fifth."
—*The Washington Post*

Swirling clockwise, in a motion
Coriolis-forced, this ocean
never stops its eastward rushin',
unaware of the discussion
that will lead to its promotion—

quite unlike (despite a notion
widely held, which experts, though, shun)
southern loos that AREN'T, when flushin',
swirling clockwise.

Will its isles (I may be gauche in
asking), due to our devotion
to our fossil fuels, grow lush in
time to see, in repercussion,
ice-melt send us (such commotion!)
swirling clockwise?

A PRACTICAL SOLUTION

"The Mercator projection is a map projection... preserving local directions and shapes. As a side effect, the Mercator projection inflates the size of objects away from the equator." Wikipedia

My lawmaker colleagues, you see on this globe
how the ice caps have shrunk; a correction
is urgently needed. Instead of a globe
I propose a Mercator projection.

WHAT REALLY MATTERS

"[Callery pears], stinky but handsome and widely popular landscape trees, have spawned aggressive invaders, creating thickets that overwhelm native plants and sport nasty four-inch spikes."
—*AP News*

So, yes, it has spikes that could skewer a possum,
like fangs from an oversized viper.
And true, every seemingly innocent blossom
spreads stench like an overripe diaper.
And granted, its canopy, blocking the light,
kills indigenous trees in our city.
And it breeds like a weed. And it's murder to fight.
On the other hand—isn't it pretty?

PART THREE: DEVOTIONAL POEMS AND HYMNS

A SOUTHERN CHRISTMAS

Of course we try to roast a bird,
make mashed potatoes, bake a pie,
and craft a coziness absurd
for Durban's dazzling summer sky.

The kitchen's claustrophobic heat,
the lounge's wilting evergreen,
the curtains' shuffling shade — all meet
to mock their artificial scene.

Forget the fir, the fire, the fife;
this season needs another sign:
a waterfront awash with life,
an ice cube melting into wine.

A CAPPELLA

Some Sundays when the church is full,
the organ summons from the hymns
embedded in our body's soul
a breath to quicken lungs and limbs.

She builds it; we, inspired, respond
and scale the scaffolding she lays
until our voices lift beyond
her loft to sound the psalm of praise.

She stops — one verse the people sing
accompanied by air alone;
her pipes, reverberating, ring
with echoes from the wood and stone.

She plays again, rejoining as
a partner in the harmony.
Her absence, like her presence, has
secured the song to set it free.

HOW LONG, O LORD

A Hymn

How long the prophets prophesied,
O Lord, your promised birth.
You came at last, You lived, You died —
You rose and raised the earth.
We fell away, You came again
In glory in Your Word,
Proclaiming there Your endless reign,
Our God and only Lord.

But still, O Lord, on floor-worn knees
We cry to rend the night:
How long until our injuries
On earth are set aright?
Deceptions and injustices
Endure on every side.
How long in such a wilderness,
O Lord, must we abide?

A time, and times, and half a time
Until the bride prepared
For union walks all lands and finds
How wrong can be repaired.
In faithful hope we seek that day,
Repenting of our sin
And working justice where we may,
While You work all within.

NEW CHURCH DAY

Let earth with heaven ever sing
the good news the apostles brought:
the Lord God Jesus Christ is King!

With angel armies following,
the Word prevailed; the truth He taught
let earth with heaven ever sing.

Still hear their anthem echoing:
"Forever over realms He's wrought
the Lord God Jesus Christ is King!"

And yet when night is darkening
I see with shame where I have not
let earth with heaven ever sing —

where I abandoned suffering
for comfort, as if I forgot
the Lord God Jesus Christ was King.

But hold, my soul, from languishing.
Awake! The battle must be fought.
Let earth with heaven ever sing:
the Lord God Jesus Christ is king!

HYMN FOR A BAPTISM

Lord, let the waters of Your Word
Wash over us and make us clean;
Teach us to cast off sin, assured
That You are with us, though unseen.

Lord, let the spirit of Your truth
Breathe wisdom into every mind,
That we may all, in age or youth,
Have light and be no longer blind.

Lord, let the fire of Your great love
Ignite within our hearts the will
To live with mercy from above
And through all trials to love You still.

HYMN FOR A WEDDING

Lord, let the pair united
In marriage ever see,
With gladdened eyes clear-sighted,
How they increasingly
May share, through changing weather,
One flesh, one mind, one heart.
Let these you join together
Be never pulled apart.

And grant Your church a vision
Of union strong and true,
A bond without division
Between Your bride and You.
In tender love and pity
Provide for us a place
Where, standing in Your city,
We see you face to face.

So let Your wisdom in us
Be married to Your love;
Let seeds You plant within us
Be showered from above
With sunshine and fresh water,
That over all the earth
Your every son and daughter
May bloom in heavenly birth.

LABOR OF LOVE

The heavens fill with smoke as campfires blaze
and actors paint themselves into their pictures
while speakers echo back the choral strains
of tracks laid down in living rooms then mixed
for these tableaux. Cars crawl down Quarry Road
past shepherd families gathered in the gloom,
past travelers barely sheltered from the cold
beside the inn, told, "Sorry, there's no room."

Eight miles away a shepherd's son, a nurse,
turns left to leave St. Joseph's Hospital,
his finished double shift among the worst
since COVID hit — breaks skipped, the ward past full,
his team a missing-membered skeleton,
outbursts, code after code. A patient dead.
He hears among the blended baritones
his own voice as he nears the church ahead.

The wise men know, and Mary, and the choir,
that all their work here won't bring on the dawn —
that they cannot supply the balm required
to give untroubled sleep to anyone
whose days and dreams of harried desperation
permit no heavenly peace, no silent night.
Only for this their weeks of preparation:
a single touch of myrrh, one tiny light.

HOW JUST, HOW LEARNED, HOW WISE

I once heard loud shouts, which seemed to gurgle up from the lower regions through waters, one toward the left, crying, "O how just!" another toward the right, "O how learned!" and a third from behind, "O how wise!" (True Christian Religion n. 332)

The seer in the spirit world
heard three exultant cries
come burbling up from lands beneath:
"How just! How learn'd! How wise!"

Toward this din he downward climbed
and saw with opened eyes
three companies each shouting praise,
"How just!" "How learn'd!" "How wise!"

He neared the clique who cried "How just!"
and saw a court of bricks
where judges sat in robes around
a fire of pitch-soaked sticks.

The judges knew each point of law
that might enrich their friends,
and skillfully they wreathed their writs
to bring about such ends.

Sulfureous phantom shapes lit up
the walls on every side,
and when each judge's verdict came,
"How just!" his friends all cried.

The seer with an angel guide
next sought the "learned" crew
and found them in a sunken plain
stamped flat by boot and shoe.

"Each scholar here," the angel said,
"Has such an open mind
he won't decide on anything
or leave one doubt behind."

"Please let me pose a question," called
the seer as he waved.
"By what religion must one live
in order to be saved?"

"Let us discuss," the scholars said,
"But first let us define
'religion' (if such thing exists).
This may take us some time."

"Some time?" the seer asked. "How long?
A day? Two weeks, or three?"
"Oh, goodness no," they said, "We'll need
at least a century."

"And in the meantime," scoffed the seer,
"You'll live just as you please."
"Indeed," they said, "and keep our pure
epistemologies!"

The scholars tramped in place again
debating long and loud,
and, as it meant *they* need not change,
"How learned!" cried the crowd.

At last the seer came to those
who shouted out, "How wise!"
and found a crowd around some men
constructing clever lies.

"They aren't lies," said one of them
when called out from the rest.
"We prove our points with solid facts —
just put me to the test."

A nearby skeptic challenged him,
"Then prove a raven's white."
"It is! The blackness that you see
is just a trick of light.

Each fiber of its feathers viewed
up close is white as snow.
You see? There's nothing true or false
but thinking makes it so."

"Then can you prove," the seer asked,
"That you have lost your mind?"
"I can, but I would rather not,"
the prudent man declined.

The perks of this approach weren't lost
on those who gathered there,
and so, in shouted unison,
"How wise!" they did declare.

So — when you tingle from acclaim
or glow in your own eyes,
be wary of the voice that cries,
"How just, how learn'd, how wise!"

MEDITATION ON THE MAGNIFICAT

All the builders up of Babel
will be scattered, kingdoms shattered,
when the King is born in pure humility;

and my pride with all its craving
to be flattered will be battered —
let it be so, Lord, and let me let it be.

FIVE PARABLES OF JESUS

I. Parable of the Good Samaritan

"But he, willing to justify himself, said unto Jesus, And who is my neighbour?" (Luke 10:29)

"*Who is…*" is not "*How can I be*
the neighbor?" Answering the first:
the truth-perverting enemy,

the woke or MAGA one, the worst
conceited centrist type, who halts
to help a man he might have cursed.

It cuts. The second answer salts:
be him — your own have graver faults.

II. Parable of the Sower

"There went out a sower to sow... Some fell by the wayside...Some fell on stony ground... Some fell among thorns...And other fell on good ground. (Mark 4:3-8)

Same seed, perhaps same soil but packed
or graveled, brambled or well-tilled —
primed to reject, flare, choke, enact.

Who failed, before the Word was spilled,
to plow, pick rocks, uproot the weed
where ready earth lies unfulfilled?

Forgive the fallow; working, plead;
prepare, as if alone, for seed.

III. Parable of the Prodigal Son

"And he said unto him, Son, thou art ever with me, and all that I have is thine. It was meet that we should make merry, and be glad: for this thy brother was dead, and is alive again; and was lost, and is found." (Luke 15:31-32)

I've been both brothers – older, younger –
annoyed by someone's half-earned praise,
ashamed of self-inflicted hunger.

The father calls me out these days —
to drop the urge to mention swine;
to find an open, blameless gaze;

to say not, "Can you *please* not whine!"
but, "Peace, my child – receive what's mine."

IV. Parable of the Pharisee and the Publican

"The Pharisee stood and prayed thus with himself, God, I thank thee, that I am not as other men are, extortioners, unjust, adulterers, or even as this publican." (Luke 18:11)

A man gave thanks for being kept
from lechery and theft and fraud.
He saw a publican who wept,

and, there but for the grace of God…
This gratitude was justified!
And neither were his habits flawed.

How could a soul so well-supplied
succumb to sin so plain as pride?

V. Parable of the Wheat and the Tares

"Let both grow together until the harvest: and in the time of harvest I will say to the reapers, 'Gather ye together first the tares, and bind them in bundles to burn them: but gather the wheat into my barn.'" (Matthew 13:30)

The field is thick with jostling stems
of wheat and weeds, as one until
the far-off harvest time condemns

the weeds and saves the wheat to mill.
For now, I'm asked a single deed:
to fight three blighted thoughts that kill —

that all is wheat; that all is weed;
that I can sense who sowed which seed.

OUTER DARKNESS

But he that had received one talent went and digged in the earth, and hid his lord's money. (Matthew 25:18)

Sure, give a handout to the guy
who begs for coins from passersby.
Pretend his story's not a lie;
be called a saint.

Or give your cash to institutes
well-staffed by stiffs in pricey suits
whose tendency to bear small fruits
they call "restraint."

Your best attempts at helping hurt.
You go ahead and give your shirt;
I'll keep my talent in the dirt,
free from taint.

WOE, WOE, WOE

We heard his word
and something stirred —
a nerve vibrating,
resonating
as if strummed
until we thrummed,
until we found
his voice's sound
had seized us fully,
left us wholly
rearranged.
We thought we changed.

INHERITANCE

And Noah began to be an husbandman, and he planted a vineyard: and he drank of the wine, and was drunken; and he was uncovered within his tent. Genesis 9:20-21

The ark will rise, the ark will fall,
and even after, we will find
our father drunk, exposing all
the foibles of a fevered mind.
What then? Will he awake to scorn
or sons and daughters fled away?
Or will he find a blanket borne
to soften the returning day?

TEMPTATION

For forty days and forty nights
the waters crash above the land
and storm clouds hide the two great lights.
An uncreation is at hand.

For forty days and forty nights
on Sinai, Moses sits in cloud
and eats no bread, nor drinks, but writes
the words that will convict the crowd.

For forty years of weary days
the manna falls, the daily bread
enduring though the people's praise
decays, and grievance grows instead.

For forty days and forty nights
the Lord endures the tempter's scorn.
Alone on desert land He fights
to see our undone souls reborn.

PALM SUNDAY

As all the wedding guests are well aware,
the bride and bridegroom's burning hearts will cool.
No couple can escape the time-worn rule:
the budding branch, come winter, must grow bare.
A cynic mocks the thought that love might spare
these two from turning cowardly or cruel;
a witness (whom the former calls a fool)
thinks frost might yet give way to warmer air.

The shouting crowd who celebrate their King
grasp little of what lauding Him will mean;
arrayed in ignorance, the children bring
abundant fronds to lay a path of green.
Within a week, the crowd will turn away.
And yet — let loud hosannas sound today.

ECCE HOMO

Behold the Man whose head is crowned
with thorny branches twisted round
by hands that bear the stain of sin.
The multitudes are pressing in
and cries of "Crucify!" resound.

Like seed sprung up in thorny ground
the loud "Hosannas" have been drowned.
Through all the frenzy and the din,
behold the Man.

Behold Him now condemned and bound.
Behold Him. Hear the hammers pound.
Behold, as well, the soldier's grin.
Behold a mirror. Look within
and face whatever there is found.
Behold the Man.

THE ROAD TO EMMAUS

On Sunday, two disciples walk
dejected till they meet a Man
who sets their hearts ablaze with talk

of Christ fulfilling Scripture's plan.
They cling to every word that's said;
though understanding, neither can

discern from speech His name; instead,
they know Him when He breaks the bread.

VINE AND BRANCHES

A Rod shall grow from Jesse's trunk,
a Stem from Jesse's root;
the woman's Seed, long prophesied,
shall prosper and bear fruit.
The people planted by the waters
weathering all strife
shall see the Source from whom they've sprung:
the loving Tree of Life.

STARSONG

Our grandfathers' grandfathers sang of the light
Of a star that would rise with a King;
They turned their eyes heavenward night after night —
But none ever saw a thing.
Now most of the world has forgotten their word
And although we remember, we feared
That neither would we see, for all we had heard,
That star. Then the star appeared.

What infant rests under its silvery gleam?
Who waits for our incense and gold?
The Light to Whom kings and all nations shall stream,
The Sunrise so long foretold.

We followed it here to Jerusalem's throne,
But the Sovereign we seek can't be found.
They say, "Search in Bethlehem"; no more is known.
Where is He, this King uncrowned?
The palace is dim. We step into the night.
Have we journeyed for nothing so far?
Then over the village there moves a small light.
It glimmers again — the star!

What infant rests under its silvery gleam?
Who waits for our incense and gold?
The Light to Whom kings and all nations shall stream,
The Sunrise so long foretold.

THE LEAST OF THESE

Teach me to feed the hungry first,
to bring a cup for those who thirst,
to gather migrant strangers in,
to clothe exposed and naked skin,
to go to homes where sickness falls,
to visit within prison walls.
In all these things I seek to do,
Lord, let me always act from You.

I long to feed on what is good,
to taste a truth not understood.
I wander, needing to be taught,
my mind stripped bare of higher thought.
I sicken — sin constricts my heart;
I'm trapped by the deceiver's art.
So may I in humility
accept the aid that's offered me.

And You, Lord — do You hunger too,
and thirst to bless with good and true?
No room was made when You were born;
at death, Your clothes were snatched and torn.
You felt the ills of humankind,
endured, then broke, the chains that bind,
became the least to offer grace —
in lowliness we see Your face.

THANKSGIVING

For moments of unmerited delight;
for toddlers on a plastic sliding board;
for lunchtime dinners lingering till night;
for everyday abundance – thank you, Lord.

ABOUT THE AUTHOR

Coleman Glenn is a New Church pastor living in Bryn Athyn, PA with his wife and their six kids (plus several chickens). His poems have appeared in *Light, Autumn Sky Poetry Daily, Blue Unicorn, THINK, Grand Little Things, Better Than Starbucks, Trinity House Review, Asses of Parnassus,* and *The Dirigible Balloon.* He is a contributing editor for *Light.*

www.ingramcontent.com/pod-product-compliance
Lightning Source LLC
Chambersburg PA
CBHW032045040426
42449CB00007B/997